Class 159s
30 Years' Service

MARK V. PIKE

BRITAIN'S RAILWAYS SERIES, VOLUME 47

Front cover image: On a perfect early summer day, 159019 is arriving at Corfe Castle with the summer Saturday-only service from Basingstoke & Salisbury (via Yeovil/Weymouth/Wareham). Is there another heritage railway in the UK with such a charming view as this? 8 June 2019.

Title page image: Leading a service from London Waterloo to Plymouth, 159021 is approaching Powderham foot crossing. 19 September 2002.

Contents page image: 159104 is running at its maximum permitted speed of 90mph past Farnborough (Main) with 1L30, the 09.18 Gillingham (Dorset) to London Waterloo service. 6 June 2016.

Back cover image: This is 159007 leading 1L41, the 14.20 London Waterloo to Exeter St Davids, into Basingstoke station. 28 January 2019.

Published by Key Books
An imprint of Key Publishing Ltd
PO Box 100
Stamford
Lincs PE9 1XQ

www.keypublishing.com

The right of Mark V. Pike to be identified as the author of this book has been asserted in accordance with the Copyright, Designs and Patents Act 1988 Sections 77 and 78.

Copyright © Mark V. Pike, 2023

ISBN 978 1 80282 359 2

All rights reserved. Reproduction in whole or in part in any form whatsoever or by any means is strictly prohibited without the prior permission of the Publisher.

Typeset by SJmagic DESIGN SERVICES, India.

Contents

Introduction 4

Chapter 1   Class 159/0 5

Chapter 2   Class 159/1 75

Introduction

Back in the late 1980s, the Class 50, and later Class 47 locomotives working Network SouthEast's West of England line from London Waterloo to Salisbury and Exeter St Davids were in dire need of quick replacement. The locomotives were never really ideal for the frequent station stops along the route, and often failed. As a result of the long sections of single track left west of Salisbury following the short-sighted Beeching cuts, just one breakdown could often create total mayhem within the timetable. Quite a few options were considered for replacement trains, including electrification of the line, short-formed HST sets and even the construction of new locomotives and stock. A study carried out came to the conclusion that the best way forward was either electrification or new DMUs. Coincidentally, it was found that train operator Regional Railways had actually ordered too many Class 158 units at the same time as Network SouthEast was looking for new trains. As a result of this development, all the above ideas were forgotten and Network SouthEast agreed to take on these surplus Class 158s, which certainly saved an awful lot of time and money designing completely new units. However, these trains never actually ran as Class 158s, being rebuilt as Class 159s by Babcock Rail in Rosyth Dockyard before entering traffic for Network SouthEast. This involved the fitting of First Class accommodation and various other refinements.

A collection of units at Salisbury. From left to right are 159019+159007+159104. 11 August 2015.

Chapter 1
Class 159/0

All the original 159/0s were intended to be constructed as Class 158s as a follow-on to an existing order, but at that time Network SouthEast were looking for something to replace unreliable loco-hauled services on the West of England line, so instead redesignated them as Class 159s. Modified and painted in Network SouthEast livery, they entered service as 159001–159022. They have also undergone a few refurbishments in their time and have now been in service for almost 30 years, providing pretty good reliability.

Right: This is the very first unit, 159001 (later *City of Exeter*), being shown off at the Bournemouth TRSMD open day. At this point it was so new that it was yet to gain a running number, and was still a little while off entering revenue-earning service. 12 September 1992.

Below: Almost exactly 29 years later, the same unit (now de-named) is seen at Salisbury as it shunts into position to become the leading unit of a London Waterloo-bound train that will arrive from Exeter St Davids a short while later. 21 September 2021.

Despite the anonymous nameboard, Crewkerne station is where 159005 *West of England Line* is arriving with 1L36, the 09.25 Exeter St Davids to London Waterloo service. 26 February 2011.

Much further east along the route, we see 159002 *City of Salisbury* heading west through Winchfield with a London Waterloo to Salisbury service. This has always been a favoured spot for photography, but has been spoiled in recent years by the placing of a signal gantry just out of shot to the bottom left. 10 June 2016.

Just west of Winchfield is Hook station, where we see 159008 leading a two-car Class 158 with 1L24, the 07.20 Yeovil Junction to London Waterloo service. 27 March 2015.

We are now at Tisbury for a couple of shots that were taken from a small occupation bridge just west of the station. Firstly, 159021 is seen approaching with 1L40, the 10.25 Exeter St Davids to London Waterloo service. 9 July 2012.

At the time the unit in the previous shot was approaching Tisbury, another unit would be waiting in the loop beyond the eastern end of the station, ready to proceed when 1L40 had passed it. With the station just about visible in the distance, 159019 recommences its journey with 1L25, the 10.20 London Waterloo to Exeter St Davids. As will become more and more obvious throughout this book, it is very hard in places to envisage this line as the double-tracked main line it once was. 9 July 2012.

Pictures taken along the West of England line rarely portray Tisbury station, possibly due to it being in a rather cramped position and with only one platform for all trains to use. This is 159008, just about to depart with 1L22, the 06.20 Honiton to Basingstoke train. This was once a double-tracked platform with a footbridge, etc, until the whole line was decimated in the late 1960s. 18 September 2014.

Back to the eastern end of the line now as we see 159013, just arrived at London Waterloo. To the left is the unusual sight of a daylight loco-hauled test train, with Direct Rail Services 37688 *Carlisle Kingmoor* waiting to depart. 17 October 2012.

159001 (formerly *City of Exeter*), leading another 159/0, is seen from the vantage point of a handy multistorey car park just west of Vauxhall, about a mile or so from Waterloo. It is heading west with 1L29, the 11.20 London Waterloo to Exeter St Davids. The area to the right, and indeed the car park on which I was located, was once the vast Southern Railway steam depot of Nine Elms, now transformed into the New Covent Garden Market. 13 August 2019.

A similar view to the previous shot, as 159012+159022 pass by with the 09.50 London Waterloo to Salisbury train. 13 August 2019.

The snow adhering to the front end of 159009 is testament to a very cold day. The first of a selection of wintry images sees the unit heading through Clapham Junction on the last leg of its journey with a service from Salisbury to London Waterloo. 27 February 2018.

About 30 miles further west, we see 159017 departing Basingstoke in a blizzard, with a Salisbury to London Waterloo service. 20 January 2010.

The white stuff tends to be a much rarer sight as you travel further west in the UK. However, the next three images show a few instances when it has occurred in the last few years. This is 159003 *Templecombe* + 159022 emerging from the gloom and snow at a foot crossing near Motcombe, between Gillingham (Dorset) and Tisbury, with a late-running Exeter St Davids to London Waterloo service. 18 January 2013.

Another Christmas card scene as 159001 *City of Exeter* leads an unidentified unit on the approach to Yeovil Junction with 1L48, the 12.25 Exeter St Davids to London Waterloo. 6 January 2010.

Gillingham (Dorset) is the location here as 159004 *Basingstoke & Deane* arrives with 1L24, the 07.11 Yeovil Pen Mill to London Waterloo train. An unidentified unit waits to depart west with a service for Exeter St Davids. The conditions actually look worse than they were on this day; later on, the snow showers cleared to reveal a lovely day! 1 March 2005.

Gillingham (Dorset) again, this time without snow as 159019 arrives with 1L30, the 09.18 Gillingham (Dorset) to Basingstoke. The unit had arrived from Basingstoke about 15 minutes earlier in the down platform. It had not long undergone another refurbishment and repaint, this time for South Western Railway (SWR). 26 September 2019.

Still at Gillingham, we see 159002 *City of Salisbury* arriving with 1L29, the 11.20 London Waterloo to Exeter St Davids service. Waiting to depart towards Salisbury is Class 43 HST power car 43062 *John Armitt*, leading the 1Q23 Old Oak Common to Salisbury via Exeter New Measurement Train, which visits this line on a roughly monthly cycle. 21 January 2010.

Since the end of 2009, the current limit of where the vast majority of trains from/to London Waterloo using the West of England line start or finish is Exeter St Davids. 159013 waits to depart at the front of 1L36, the 09.25 Exeter St Davids to London Waterloo. 8 October 2019.

The first stop from St Davids is Exeter Central, which was a very busy location back in the days of steam and originally had two through lines. Nowadays there are just two tracks remaining, with a single bay platform that is rarely used. Seen again prior to receiving SWR livery, 159013 is departing with 1L40, the 10.25 Exeter St Davids to London Waterloo. 16 April 2015.

Turning to look in the other direction on the same bridge from which the last image was taken, we see 159010 approaching with a slightly late-running 1L13, the 07.10 London Waterloo to Exeter St Davids. 24 March 2011.

The City of Salisbury is situated more or less midway between London Waterloo and Exeter, and as such is always a good place to view Class 159 activity. The station itself is well known for hardly changing throughout its existence. This is original Network SouthEast-liveried 159015, arriving with a service from London Waterloo to Exeter St Davids. The severity of the curve here can be appreciated from this view. 26 February 2000.

Just over 21 years later, 159015 is now in SWR livery. It is seen here shunting into position in Platform 2, ready to form the front portion of a service from Exeter St Davids. To the right of this view can be seen the original water tower, a relic from steam days, and also the frontage of the original GWR station that was originally a terminus on a separate line from Warminster and Westbury. This situation changed in 1932 when the GWR station was closed; all GWR services subsequently used the main SR station, as they do to this day. The former GWR station buildings were, however, listed in 1972 and exist today as non-railway office units. 30 March 2021.

Entering the bay Platform 6 at the eastern end of the station is 159020, arriving as ECS to form 1L54, the 15.47 Salisbury to London Waterloo. In times past, this was the main platform for trains using the long-closed line to Bournemouth via West Moors and Ringwood. 17 February 2022.

159005 (formerly *West of England Line*) arrives at Platform 3 with 1L37, the 13.20 London Waterloo to Exeter St Davids. 1 April 2019.

Departing from the same platform as in the previous shot, this is 159003 (formerly *Templecombe*) after coming off the rear of 1L29, the 11.20 London Waterloo to Exeter St Davids. The unit will now either proceed to Salisbury Depot for servicing, or form the front portion of another service for London Waterloo. 25 July 2022.

There are times when things all come together to form a unique picture. This was the case here as we see 159005 (formerly *West of England Line*) slowly heading down the reception line that will give it access to the depot for servicing. A huge shower had just passed, and this perfect rainbow appeared, just for a few minutes. Right place at the right time! 27 August 2020.

We now head further east again, to the South Western Main Line at Totters Lane, between Hook and Winchfield, where 159002 *City of Salisbury* approaches with 1L34, the 10.47 Salisbury to London Waterloo train. The section between Basingstoke and Waterloo is where the limited 90mph capability of these units can often affect timings, especially if running late. 2 September 2010.

To the left is a glimpse of the bridge from which the previous image was taken as 159004 *Basingstoke & Deane* passes by with 1L44, the 11.25 Exeter St Davids to London Waterloo. Note the two World War Two pillboxes still in situ either side of the line. 2 September 2010.

Currently the longest length of train that operates between London and Salisbury is a 10-car formation, consisting of two Class 159s and two two-car Class 158s. A couple of these combinations run during the day, usually at peak times. This is 159007, leading 1L21, the 09.20 London Waterloo to Exeter St Davids, on the approach to Farnborough (Main). This formation would have worked an early morning service up from Exeter/Salisbury. Upon arrival at Salisbury, the leading one or two units would continue on to Exeter St Davids and the two Class 158s would probably head to the depot. 12 September 2019.

This time, we see 159021 leading a London Waterloo to Salisbury service through the freshly re-laid track on the down fast line at Farnborough (Main). 12 December 2006.

This is the western end of Farnborough (Main) as we see 159003 (formerly *Templecombe*) leading 1L25, the 10.20 London Waterloo to Exeter St Davids service. This shot was taken from the former parcels handling platform, closed back in the late 1960s and now a car park. 23 March 2022.

Turning the camera the other way, we capture a very clean 159022 approaching on the front of 1L32, the 08.23 Exeter St Davids to London Waterloo. The front ends of these units do have a tendency to get very dirty, but this one has obviously had a good clean recently. 23 March 2022.

Woking is an important station on the West of England route, with most trains calling there. 159006 *THE SEATON TRAMWAY Seaton–Colyford–Colyton* leads 1L21, the 09.20 London Waterloo to Exeter St Davids service, away from the station. The line to Portsmouth (via Guildford) diverges to the right of the picture. Also, in the distance the regular Merehead to Woking stone train has just arrived. 15 November 2013.

The impressive and imposing Woking signal box was commissioned in June 1937, remaining in use for just over 60 years until its operation was taken over by the Woking Signalling Control Centre scheme in August 1997. It is now a listed building, and I believe the original frame and a few other fittings still remain in place. 159009 pulls away past the box with 1L19, the 08.50 London Waterloo to Salisbury train. 10 October 2013.

Heading back west, we are now at the once complex junction at Templecombe, which originally boasted no fewer than five signal boxes in its early days. The first of a few images from here sees 159010, arriving past an almost miniaturised version of Woking signal box, on the rear of an Exeter St Davids to London Waterloo service. 30 September 2008.

Viewed from the footbridge that originally stood at Buxted station in East Sussex, 159008, leading an Exeter St Davids to London Waterloo service, slows for the station stop. The commencement of double-track line to Yeovil Junction can be seen in the distance beyond the station. Since re-opening, the station itself has won awards for presentation and appearance, and in the summer is enhanced with flower planters and hanging baskets, as seen here. 17 August 2005.

With a view of the footbridge from which the previous shot was taken, this is 159009, arriving with the 10.20 London Waterloo to Exeter St Davids service. As can be seen, the former down platform is still in place, but due to certain infrastructure constraints, the up platform was the one that originally had to be reused in 1983. 30 September 2008.

Arriving from the west some eleven years later is 159008 again, this time with 1L36, the 09.25 Exeter St Davids to London Waterloo service. The signal box here opened a year later than Woking in May 1938, being positioned where the signaller had a good view of the once large goods yards either side of the main running lines and the junction between the Somerset and Dorset Joint Railway (S&DJR) platform and the main lines. The yards are all long since vanished. When the station itself closed in 1967, only this box remained on a bare platform, with all other buildings demolished. From this date, it controlled in the eastbound direction along the single track to Gillingham, and westbound along the double track as far as Yeovil Junction. In 1983, when Templecombe station was reopened, the box was virtually split in two, with half of it modified to act as a ticket office and the other half as a signal box. One member of staff thus acted as both signaller and ticket office clerk. This situation continued until the whole signalling system on the line between Salisbury and Exeter was modernised during 2011-12, with all control moving to a new signalling centre at Basingstoke. This was commissioned in March 2012, rendering most of the line's signal boxes redundant; they were decommissioned and, in some cases, demolished. Nowadays, the station is looked after by a group of local volunteers, who have also erected the running-in board seen here to reflect the station's illustrious past. Notice also the new platform installed in the foreground. 18 April 2016.

Upon resignalling in 2012, the platform situation became a bit of a problem, as no staff were employed here from that date. As a result, persons using a wheelchair or those who could not use the footbridge for any reason were effectively left marooned, prevented from exiting the station! This was rectified by installing a new platform next to the existing unused down platform. This meant that the footbridge (and the up platform) became redundant. In hindsight, one has to wonder if it would not have been more sensible to just replace the track in the existing down platform and upgrade the facilities. This new platform is, however, thought to be semi-temporary, and could easily be removed if that scenario ever happens. With the new platform not long opened and seen to the left, this is 159019 arriving with 1L60, the 15.25 Exeter St Davids to London Waterloo. 3 September 2012.

The last shot at Templecombe shows an unidentified unit arriving on the rear of a London Waterloo to Exeter St Davids service. The station itself is just out of sight to the left of shot. Any reader that might feel tempted to imbibe at the establishment in the foreground will now be disappointed to know that it is, unfortunately, no longer a public house! 24 March 2012.

Although the whole class is invariably to be found working on the West of England line, some members have occasionally strayed from there. This was the case in summer 2009, when 159008 was used in passenger service for just one day on the branch line from Brockenhurst to Lymington Pier, of all places. This little-known occurrence was also used to check clearances, etc, for the forthcoming use of two-car Class 158s on the line. This arrangement commenced on weekdays only at first (with Class 450 EMUs at weekends) and remained in place from 2010–18. Since then, Class 450s have been the sole trains to use the line. This is the first of a few images showing the only known occasion that a 159 has worked on the branch to date. The unit is seen here departing Brockenhurst as it heads down to Lymington. 17 July 2009.

Since the early 1970s, the start of the Lymington Branch has been along a separate line from Brockenhurst station, but a mile or so from the previous image is the site of Lymington Junction, from where it originally left the main line. The route to Bournemouth, Poole and Weymouth is to the right here as 159008 comes off the single line from Lymington towards Brockenhurst. Up to the late 1960s, this used to be a three-way junction, with the Lymington line diverging from the main line at this point. Just out of sight, to the right of picture, was the commencement of the 'old road', as it was known, to Poole, via Ringwood & Wimborne; it closed in 1964. A signal box to control this junction once stood almost exactly where the trackside electrical substation is in the background. 17 July 2009.

Passengers are seen boarding at the only intermediate station at Lymington Town as the unit forms a service to Brockenhurst. For a period between 1956 and 1989, however, there existed the former Ampress Works Halt near Lymington, which served a since-closed engineering firm. Interestingly, this single-platform halt was never advertised in public timetables and is extant to this day. It is hard to envisage now, but the station here at Lymington Town once boasted an overall roof up until the late 1960s. 17 July 2009.

This six-mile branch line in the heart of the New Forest National Park is perhaps better known as being the last branch to be operated by steam traction in the UK, right up until early April 1967. With the last loco that worked it (Ivatt Class 2 2-6-2T 41312) still surviving in preservation, there have been various murmurings over the years about recreating this event, but to date, nothing has come of it. The highlight of the line is the viaduct that crosses the Lymington River, between Town and Pier stations. Glimpsed amongst the mass of boats in Lymington Marina, 159008 negotiates the viaduct on its way to the Pier station. 17 July 2009.

The unit has just departed Pier station, which is just out of view to the right, and heads another service back to Brockenhurst. 17 July 2009.

For the last shot taken on this unique day, we see the unit departing from the end of the line at Lymington Pier with a service for Brockenhurst. One of the Isle of Wight ferries can be seen waiting to depart in the background, this being the main reason why the branch managed to survive the Beeching cuts of the mid-1960s. Originally there was a run-round loop for locos here, but that has long since been removed. 17 July 2009.

Back to the West of England now. Although just a shadow of its former self, Yeovil Junction is one of the larger stations on the West of England line and is where we see the next series of shots. This first one sees 159001 (formerly *City of Exeter*) in its latest SWR livery departing with 1L48, the 12.25 Exeter St Davids to London Waterloo service. The train is departing from what is now the main platform for eastbound departures; this used to be a loop platform, mainly for stopping trains and those taking the line to Yeovil Pen Mill and the now long-closed Yeovil Town stations. 17 December 2018.

Viewed from the eastern end of the long-closed former down platform, 159005 (formerly *West of England Line*) is arriving with 1L29, the 11.20 London Waterloo to Exeter St Davids service. The gate in the foreground is the entrance to the Yeovil Railway Centre, which occasionally receives steam locos off charter trains for servicing, etc. 27 February 2009.

At the opposite end of the station, we see 159018 arriving from the west with 1L56, the 14.25 Exeter St Davids to London Waterloo service. 13 April 2018.

When the units were new in the early 1990s, a handful received names associated with the line on which they were operating. I have always had an interest in names/nameplates, and they always added a bit of individuality to the locos/units, etc., to which they were applied. Unfortunately, after the first four units were named during the mid-1990s, this policy fizzled out where the 159s were concerned until units 005+006 were named in the early 2010s. 159005 is seen here at the former down platform (now maintained by the Yeovil Railway Centre), waiting for its dedication to commence. This was the penultimate unit to be named before SWR took over the franchise, and the company seemed to be little interested in namings thereafter. 23 June 2012.

The new nameplate on unit 159005 is revealed as *West of England Line*. 23 June 2012.

A hint of the station's former past is seen here with one of the two through lines still in situ but these days only occasionally used as a run-round loop for charter/engineers' trains. The station is wonderfully situated on a long sweeping curve and was, by all accounts, an excellent place to view non-stop steam-hauled trains travelling at around 60-70mph in either direction many years ago. 159019, leading 1L21, the 09.20 London Waterloo to Exeter St Davids, draws to a halt at what used to be the main up platform. 27 February 2019.

Back to the western end of the station, we see 159020 arriving with 1L28, the 07.25 Exeter St Davids to London Waterloo service. The big attraction to be found at the Yeovil Railway Centre is the original loco turntable left in situ from BR days, one of very few in the UK extant. With a fine patch of tulips bursting into bloom, the turntable is seen in the foreground, whilst on the right behind the train can be seen the former stationmaster's house. 16 April 2015.

Eight years earlier, 159020 is departing the eastern end of the station with 1L48, the 12.25 Exeter St Davids to London Waterloo. This view was taken from the former east signal box that was demolished in 2012 upon resignalling of the area. In the background can be seen an HST, which was being diverted due to engineering works on the line between Castle Cary and Exeter. 28 January 2007.

Left: Pointing the camera in the opposite direction from the signal box, we see 159021 leading a slightly late-running 1L25, the 10.20 London Waterloo to Exeter St Davids. The train is passing over the Yeovil Pen Mill to Weymouth line, denoted by the railings at the rear of the train. 28 January 2007.

Below: Prior to 2009, some London Waterloo to Exeter St Davids services extended to either Paignton or Plymouth. This series of images depicts some of these trains west of Exeter. In original Network SouthEast livery, 159011 is captured leading a South West Trains (SWT) example through Dawlish Warren with 1L65, the 10.35 London Waterloo to Paignton service. 2 May 2000.

Four years later and now in SWT livery, 159011 is seen at the same spot at Dawlish Warren, but photographed from the opposite platform. It is leading the 08.35 London Waterloo to Paignton service. 16 August 2004.

Here we see 159017, leading an unidentified westbound service for either Paignton or Plymouth on its way around the sea wall on the approach to Starcross. The awful fence was erected in the mid-2000s and detracts from an otherwise fine view. 21 October 2006.

On a rather dull afternoon, 159002 *City of Salisbury* is leading this time, as another unidentified westbound service passes along Marine Parade at Dawlish. 5 August 2001.

A broadside view of 159005 (formerly *West of England Line*) as it passes the well-known location of Cockwood Harbour, near Starcross, with a Paignton to London Waterloo service. This is another spot that has since had that awful fence erected by the lineside. 5 October 2003.

159014 again, this time coming around the sharp curve and passing Starcross station with a train from Plymouth to London Waterloo. 21 October 2006.

Another good viewpoint in the same vicinity as the last shot was the foot crossing (since replaced by a footbridge) at Powderham, just east of Starcross. The view in both directions from here was excellent, but is now even better from the footbridge. This is 159014, approaching with a Paignton to London Waterloo service. 29 September 2001.

And approaching from the east on the same day as the previous image is 159015, leading a westbound service for Plymouth. 29 September 2001.

Heading west at Dawlish is 159017, with a London Waterloo to Plymouth service. A glimpse of the long-closed signal box can be seen to the left. Despite this box being a listed building, it was demolished in the mid-2000s, as it was deemed dangerous to persons on the platform. The early 2020s have seen major modification works here; the rebuilding of the sea wall includes a completely remodelled platform on the down side, and a new footbridge will eventually be installed, approximately over where the first coach is in this view. 6 August 2001.

Seven years later, we see 159017 again at Dawlish. This time it is departing past Marine Parade with a service for Paignton. The sea wall at this point has already been rebuilt. 30 August 2008.

An unusual view of original Network SouthEast-liveried 159021, approaching Kennaway Tunnel at Dawlish as it works a Paignton to London Waterloo service. 5 August 2001.

To conclude this series of shots west of Exeter, we see 159021 again, this time leading a service from London Waterloo to Plymouth. It is approaching Powderham foot crossing. 19 September 2002.

To return to the 159s' usual operating area, we are now at the long-closed location of Semley station, which is situated at the top of a climb in both directions from Gillingham (Dorset) to the west, and from Tisbury from the east. This is 159002 (formerly *City of Salisbury*) passing by with 1L44, the 11.25 Exeter St Davids to London Waterloo. The area to the right of shot was formerly the station goods yard, and the old goods shed can still be glimpsed in the background. Not visible in this view, however, behind the bushes just to the left of the goods shed, are the substantial remains of the station buildings, which are now a private residence. Even the signal box, closed in the late 1960s, still stands. 18 August 2021.

Looking in the opposite direction on the same day as in the previous image, we see 159005 (formerly *West of England Line*) coming up the gradient towards Tisbury and Salisbury, leading 1L25, the 10.20 London Waterloo to Exeter St Davids service. More of the goods yard that was once located to the left can be seen here. 18 August 2021.

Same bridge, same direction, but this is the view from the other side as 159001 *City of Exeter* passes with 1L25, the 10.20 London Waterloo to Exeter St Davids again. Many of these services now get very overcrowded even with six-coach formations, especially in the summer months, and the use of just a single three-car unit for such a long-distance journey should really be a thing of the past in this day and age. 11 August 2011.

Unlike the halcyon days of the 1950s and 1960s, where immaculate line sides were normal, vegetation has been allowed to run riot and is now at a stage where in places it is difficult to even see the line, much less try to get unhindered photographs. I did, however, manage to find this small opening on the gradient about half a mile east of Semley, where we see 159011 leading 1L21, the 09.20 London Waterloo to Exeter St Davids train. A rare steam-hauled charter was following this train a short while later, headed by Bulleid 'Battle of Britain' Pacific 34067 *Tangmere*, which looked fantastic getting to grips with the incline! 20 April 2013.

We now move on to the unlikely location of the Swanage Railway heritage line, which in recent years has been visited by various charter trains including ones worked by Class 159s. This is 159004 *Basingstoke & Deane* after arrival at Swanage with 1Z61, the 09.16 Salisbury to Swanage UK Railtours-organised 'The Swanage Lifeboatman' charity charter. 8 May 2014.

159004 *Basingstoke & Deane* worked back to Salisbury that evening, but it is seen here exiting the station to be stabled for the day. On the left is earlier Southern Region motive power in the form of Bulleid Pacific 34028 *Eddystone*. 8 May 2014.

A few years later, SWR announced a brand new service from Basingstoke to Corfe Castle on summer Saturdays. These trains were noteworthy for involving a record number of reversals for any scheduled service; once at Yeovil Junction, again at Yeovil Pen Mill, then again at Weymouth (where the five- or six-coach formation split) and once more at Wareham, with the reverse procedure on the return. Due to industrial action at the time, these trains actually ran on far fewer Saturdays than was originally intended, and after a couple of seasons they were pulled altogether. Although running for just a short period, they are greatly missed by the people of West Wilts, North Dorset and Somerset, who now once again have no direct train to the resort of Weymouth or the Swanage Railway, or indeed the South Coast. I managed to travel on a couple of them and they were more or less packed to the rafters. On the second Saturday of operation, this is a very clean 159003 (formerly *Templecombe*) at the wonderfully restored Corfe Castle station. 2 June 2018.

Upon arrival at Corfe Castle with the train from Salisbury, the unit then formed a couple of shuttle services to Wareham and back to Corfe Castle before working 1L66, the 15.45 Corfe Castle to London Waterloo via Weymouth (to rejoin the other unit left there on the outward run). It then returned to Salisbury and Waterloo via the reverse of the outward trip. This is another view of 159003 (formerly *Templecombe*) at Corfe Castle station. 2 June 2018.

The magnificent ruins of Corfe Castle provide a grand place to view proceedings at Corfe station, and indeed the surrounding area. 159003 (formerly *Templecombe*) is seen again shunting in the station. 2 June 2018.

Just over a year later and 159019 was on duty, seen here arriving on a perfect early summer day at Corfe Castle with the service from Salisbury. Is there another heritage railway in the UK with such a charming view as this? 8 June 2019.

159019 is seen again during a shunt manoeuvre at Corfe Castle.
8 June 2019.

As mentioned earlier, the Salisbury to Corfe Castle service involved a reversal and unit detachment/attachment at Weymouth. This is 159018 at Weymouth, waiting to head to Wareham and Swanage with what turned out to be one of the last runs of the service.
14 September 2019.

We are now in the London area, to start a series of images depicting a whistlestop trip down the line to Gillingham (Dorset). Starting a few miles out of Waterloo, we see 159009 passing Vauxhall with 1L25, the 10.20 London Waterloo to Exeter St Davids service. Sadly, the view of Big Ben and the Houses of Parliament in the background is no longer possible due to tree growth.
11 September 2008.

Something that doesn't happen (or rarely happens) nowadays is the stabling of 159 units in the carriage sidings at Clapham Junction, as most services arrive at London Waterloo and form a service back south in just a short turn-round time. This is 159002 *City of Salisbury*, exiting the sidings at Clapham Junction to make for London Waterloo. 14 September 2007.

The amazing 1930s-designed Modernist station at Surbiton is seen to good effect here as 159022 leads an unidentified service for London Waterloo. The significance of the building was recognised when the station was Grade II listed in 1983. 10 December 2008.

159003 *Templecombe* is seen here passing Wimbledon West Junction leading 1L24, the 07.20 Yeovil Junction to London Waterloo service. On this very busy section of line it is often tricky to get just the one train in view! 8 September 2016.

Looking a little lost running as a three-car unit, 159010 is passing West Byfleet with a Salisbury to London Waterloo service. 5 November 2010.

This time we see 159014 leading a two-car Class 158 through the up fast line at Winchfield with 1L24, the 07.20 Yeovil Junction to London Waterloo service. The Class 158s joined SWT (now SWR) in the late 2000s and are used alongside the 159s. 23 September 2016.

159010 is seen again, this time approaching Hook station with 1L42, the 12.47 Salisbury to Basingstoke service which, since the date of this shot, has been revised to terminate at Basingstoke, as do many other services that start from Salisbury. 16 May 2019.

Just east of Basingstoke we see a full nine-car formation led by 159005 (formerly *West of England Line*) with 1L24, the 07.11 Yeovil Pen Mill to London Waterloo service, although just the rear unit would have originated at Yeovil, joining the other two at Salisbury. Basingstoke Barton Hill carriage sidings can just be seen in the distance. 1 September 2020.

Approaching the stop at Basingstoke is 159012, leading 1L29, the 11.20 London Waterloo to Exeter St Davids service. 12 January 2022.

Unfortunately, they don't stay like this for long! Ex-works 159002 (formerly *City of Salisbury*) leads a late running 1V27, the 10.50 London Waterloo to Salisbury train. This service now starts from Basingstoke and terminates at Yeovil Junction. 12 September 2019.

Still at Basingstoke, but this is the up siding, which very rarely sees any visits from Class 159s. On this particular day, engineering works in the area necessitated the use of this siding. 159017 is seen departing, whilst 159011 is stabled in the distance. 12 January 2022.

A few miles west of Basingstoke is Worting Junction, where the lines to Southampton and Weymouth, and to Salisbury and Exeter part company. This is 159001 *City of Exeter* leading 1L33, the 12.20 London Waterloo to Exeter St Davids service. 13 March 2017.

Looking west at Worting Junction, we see 159010 leading 1L28, the 07.25 Exeter St Davids to London Waterloo service. Battledown Flyover, which takes the London-bound up line from Southampton over the West of England line, is in the distance. 18 March 2019.

Viewed across the field this time, we see 159014+159004 *Basingstoke & Deane* is approaching Battledown Flyover with the 10.50 London Waterloo to Salisbury service. 14 February 2009.

With a fine view of the flyover, 159019 dives beneath it whilst, leading 1L31, the 11.50 London Waterloo to Salisbury service. This was a very popular location back in the days of steam as well as now. 5 April 2016.

We are now at Whitchurch (Hants) as we head off down the line towards Salisbury. Approaching the station is 159003 *Templecombe* leading 1L44, the 11.25 Exeter St Davids to London Waterloo. 25 January 2015.

Right: Heading in the opposite direction is 159018 with 1L29, the 11.20 London Waterloo to Exeter St Davids. The new-looking bridge dominating this image was rebuilt in the early 2010s for the slightly higher container wagons that are used on this section of line, mainly as a diversionary route. 25 January 2015.

Below: This is 159011 leading 1L36, the 09.25 Exeter St Davids to London Waterloo. 25 January 2015.

About a mile or so west of Whitchurch is the graceful nine-arch viaduct at Hurstbourne Priors, where we see 159001 *City of Exeter* leading 1L41, the 14.20 London Waterloo to Exeter St Davids service. 21 February 2015.

Between Whitchurch and Andover there are some long, deep cuttings hewn from the chalk in this area. 159011 has just entered one of these cuttings, four miles east of Andover station, with 1L34, the 10.47 Salisbury to London Waterloo train. 21 February 2013.

Andover is another once-busy junction station on the route and is our next location. Here we see 159022 leading a ten-car formation that makes up 1L19, the 08.50 London Waterloo to Salisbury service. It is quite obvious from looking at this shot that the station once boasted up and down through lines. It was also situated more or less mid-way along the former Midland and South Western Junction Railway, which ran from Cheltenham via Swindon/Andover/Romsey to Southampton Terminus but has long since vanished, apart from a small section from Andover to Ludgershall that sees occasional use to this day, for military purposes. 12 March 2015.

The bridge from which I took the previous shot is in the background as we see, to the left, 159008 with 1L31, the 11.50 London Waterloo to Salisbury, and to the right, 159018 leading 1L42, the 12.47 Salisbury to London Waterloo service. 15 March 2014.

Looking in the other direction from the footbridge on which I took the previous shot, we see 159008 arriving with 1L31, the 11.50 London Waterloo to Salisbury.
15 March 2014.

Approaching the platform at Andover is 159006 (formerly *THE SEATON TRAMWAY Seaton-Colyford-Colyton*) with 1V27, the 10.50 London Waterloo to Yeovil Junction. The aforementioned Midland and South Western Junction Railway used to diverge off to the right behind the grey cabinet towards Andover Town and Romsey.
8 September 2021.

Looking west towards Salisbury, we see 159022 approaching with 1L34, the 10.47 Salisbury to London Waterloo. The remaining small section of the former cross-country route mentioned previously now extends just to Ludgershall MOD, leaving the main line behind the train.
12 March 2015.

Looking east from the bridge seen in the background of the previous shot, we see 159011 leading 1V23, the 09.50 London Waterloo to Yeovil Junction service. This unit was one of the early recipients of SWR livery, with the silver being a darker shade and featuring the diagonal stripes along the bodyside that were omitted in later repaints. 20 September 2018.

The final view at Andover is taken from the same bridge as in the previous view, but this time looking west as 159002 *City of Salisbury* leads 1L36, the 09.25 Exeter St Davids to London Waterloo service. The Ludgershall branch can be seen to the right; it follows the main line for about a mile or so before veering away. 12 March 2015.

The only intermediate station now remaining between Andover and Salisbury is Grateley, mainly served by the Salisbury to Basingstoke/London Waterloo semi-fast services. Speeding through the station is 159018, leading 1L32, the 08.23 Exeter St Davids to London Waterloo. The footbridge in view here was originally to be found further west, at Whimple. 1 November 2017.

About a mile west of Grateley, at a location known as Palestine, we see 159017 leading 1L22, the 06.20 Honiton to London Waterloo service. 23 March 2013.

We have now reached the outskirts of Salisbury at Tunnel Junction, where 159007 leads 1L40, the 10.25 Exeter St Davids to London Waterloo service. This is the site of the unfortunate accident that occurred on 31 October 2021, when 159102 collided with the rear of a GWR Class 158 as it entered the tunnel mouth seen in this view. Bad rail head conditions were to blame, and thankfully no passengers were seriously injured, although the driver of the Class 159 did spend a few days in hospital. 3 April 2015.

As we visited Salisbury station earlier in this chapter, we now move further west to see 159008 climbing out of the station with 1L25, the 10.20 London Waterloo to Exeter St Davids. Behind the train and to the right is the location of the large former Salisbury steam depot, which closed with the end of steam in 1967. Dominating the skyline in the background is the unmistakeable spire of Salisbury Cathedral which, at 123m (404ft), is the tallest in the UK. 18 January 2006.

There are clues here again that this was once a double-tracked main line route as we arrive at the long-closed station at Dinton, between Wilton Junction and Tisbury. What is also obvious is the rampant forest-like growth of trees along the lineside, which has become even worse in recent years. 159021 is approaching with 1L44, the 11.25 Exeter St Davids to London Waterloo service. Despite the many years that have passed since closure, Dinton station is actually still quite intact, with the main station now in private ownership. 16 October 2008.

Summer 2022 was probably best known for the nationwide drought, with many days going by without rain. A result of this was that a section of embankment on the West of England line between Tisbury and Gillingham (Dorset) became unstable, forcing Network Rail to impose a severe speed restriction. As this is a single line, the timetable had to be adjusted to try and keep timings in order. Near to the section concerned and just after the restriction had been lifted, this is 159009+159015, passing the small hamlet of Semley with a late-running 1L29, the 11.20 London Waterloo to Exeter St Davids. 7 December 2022.

An unidentified 159/0 departs Tisbury with 1L68, the 17.25 Exeter St Davids to London Waterloo train. The huge thatched tithe barn prominent in the picture once belonged to Shaftesbury Abbey, founded by King Alfred in 888 AD. It dates from the 13th Century, and the roof is believed to be the largest expanse of thatch in the UK. 28 April 2011.

With a sort of half-hearted attempt at lineside clearance having recently taken place, this is 159005 (formerly *West of England Line*) passing near the village of Motcombe on the approach to Gillingham (Dorset), leading 1L53, the 17.23 London Waterloo to Exeter St Davids service. 26 April 2012.

WEST OF ENGLAND LINE

We have now reached Gillingham (Dorset), where we see 159003 (formerly *Templecombe*) about to depart with 1L37, the 13.20 London Waterloo to Exeter St Davids. This was the first unit to receive the SWR livery, and has the (later abandoned) diagonal stripes along the bodysides. 11 April 2018.

Just before sunset, near to the shortest day of the year, 159022 arrives at Gillingham (Dorset) with 1L56, the 14.25 Exeter St Davids to London Waterloo. The single siding seen here is retained for the use of stabling the occasional track machine. 16 December 2011.

Earlier in this chapter, we saw some images of units visiting the Swanage Railway. This is 159011 at the same spot as the previous image, arriving at Gillingham (Dorset) with 1L66, the 15.45 Corfe Castle to London Waterloo via Weymouth and Salisbury. 30 June 2018.

Up until December 2021, another regular route for the class was from Salisbury to Bristol. This is 159013 arriving at Bristol Temple Meads with 1V22, the 10.57 Salisbury to Bristol Temple Meads, which started out as the rear portion of 1L21, the 09.20 London Waterloo to Exeter St Davids that split at Salisbury. 3 December 2018.

Right: The same service as seen in the previous image is this time arriving at Bath Spa, on this occasion with 159017. 5 September 2018.

Below: In some fine autumn sunshine and colours, 159004 *Basingstoke & Deane* is seen approaching the stop at Freshford, in the picturesque Avon Valley between Bath and Trowbridge, with 1O32, the 08.51 Bristol Temple Meads to Salisbury. This would then attach to the rear of 1L32, the 08.24 Exeter to London Waterloo at Salisbury, to continue through to its destination. 17 November 2011.

About a couple of miles or so from where the previous shot was taken, this is 159001 *City of Exeter* about to pass beneath the Dundas Aqueduct with 1V22, the 10.57 Salisbury to Bristol Temple Meads service. It was close to here that scenes were filmed for the famous 1953 film *The Titfield Thunderbolt*. 12 April 2014.

On the outskirts of Westbury at Heywood Village, just south of Trowbridge, we see 159009 passing a fine patch of Rosebay Willowherb with 1O32, the 08.51 Bristol Temple Meads to Salisbury service. 10 July 2018.

About a half a mile further south from the last image is Hawkeridge Junction, where we see 159022 passing with 1V22, the 10.57 Salisbury to Bristol Temple Meads service. The lines diverging to the left bypass Westbury station; they are mainly used for freight trains and, occasionally, diverted service trains.
6 March 2015.

This time 159001 *City of Exeter* is seen awaiting departure from Westbury with 1O48, the 12.51 from Bristol Temple Meads to Salisbury, where it would attach to 1L48, the 12.25 Exeter St Davids to London Waterloo service.
16 May 2008.

Another shot at Westbury, this time 159012 in ex-works SWR livery on its return run to Salisbury Traction and Rolling Stock Maintenance Depot (T&SRMD) from refurbishment at Brush Works at Loughborough.
24 January 2019.

Heading south now from Westbury on the route to Salisbury through the Wylye Valley, 159002 *City of Salisbury* is topping the incline at Upton Scudamore with 1O48, the 12.51 from Bristol Temple Meads to Salisbury. The fierce incline from Westbury has always been difficult for heavy trains, with many requiring a banking loco even as recently as the 1990s. 18 July 2014.

A few miles further south than the previous shot, 159005 (later *West of England Line*) passes Little Langford with 1V33, the 13.52 Salisbury to Bristol Temple Meads service. This had detached at Salisbury from the rear of 1L33, the 12.20 London Waterloo to Exeter St Davids. 19 March 2009.

During the final year that SWR served Bristol, this is 159005 (formerly *West of England Line*) now in SWR livery at almost the same spot taken from the bridge in the previous image, with a late-running 1V21, the 10.57 Salisbury to Bristol Temple Meads. This detached at Salisbury from the rear of 1L21, the 09.20 London Waterloo to Exeter St Davids. 16 June 2021.

Class 159s are now regularly seen on services to/from Yeovil Pen Mill. Presently there are a couple of trains originating/terminating at London Waterloo that are routed via the line through the Wylye Valley that we saw in the previous shot. From Westbury, they then take the line to Taunton/Exeter/Plymouth as far as Castle Cary, from where they diverge to Yeovil. This route has also often been used for route learning/driver training and diverted services. The bright yellow rapeseed growing in the field is a giveaway to the time of year, as 159005 (formerly *West of England Line*) is seen again on a crew training run from Salisbury to Yeovil Junction (via Castle Cary) soon after departing Westbury. 22 May 2018.

159005 (formerly *West of England Line*) is obviously a regular here as it is seen again from the same position as the previous shot but looking west as it approaches with another crew trainer from Yeovil Junction to Salisbury. 14 May 2019.

A few miles further west, we see 159009 at Berkeley Marsh, near Frome, with the Saturday 09.50 Yeovil Junction to London Waterloo service. 13 September 2020.

The next station down the line is Castle Cary, from where the line to Yeovil leaves the main line to the West Country. This is 159010 arriving with 1V35, the 13.50 Waterloo to Yeovil Pen Mill service, which has now unfortunately ceased running. 11 October 2016.

Still further west, 159022 is arriving at Bruton with 1O40, the 10.44 Yeovil Pen Mill to London Waterloo. Strangely, the building behind the loco, looking remarkably like a signal box, is nothing to do with the railway and never has been! It was built quite recently and is actually part of a car maintenance garage. The designer obviously had some sort of affinity with the railway! 21 July 2021.

The unusual double-faced platform at Yeovil Pen Mill is seen to good effect here as 159014 passes through with a route/crew learning special. Only the left-hand side is used for northbound trains, whilst the platform to the right is used for southbound services. 18 December 2003.

Arriving at its destination past the signal box, which is still in use in 2023, this is 159009 with 1V35, the 13.50 Waterloo to Yeovil Pen Mill service. 4 October 2017.

Above: We now head back to the West of England line again. A few miles west of Gillingham (Dorset) lies the long-favourite spot for generations of photographers at Buckhorn Weston Tunnel, sometimes known as Gillingham Tunnel. 159001 *City of Exeter* approaches from the east, leading 1L17, the 08.20 London Waterloo to Exeter St Davids service. This view has now been totally ruined by the placing of a large radio mast slap bang in the right foreground. 27 August 2009.

Left: A far better view can be had by looking west towards the tunnel. 159016 is passing with a Yeovil Junction to London Waterloo service. There have been a few landslips in the tunnel area, so the cutting sides are now kept free from undergrowth. 4 July 2019.

At the same spot as the previous shot, but this time from an angle not normally seen, 159010 leads 1L68, the 17.25 Exeter St Davids to London Waterloo service. 7 May 2016.

Looking at this shot, it is perhaps hard to believe that a double-track main line used to run through this tunnel. 159006 (*THE SEATON TRAMWAY Seaton-Colyford-Colyton*) is exiting with 1L36, the 09.25 Exeter St Davids to London Waterloo service. 27 August 2009.

Not often photographed, however, is the western end of the same tunnel. With a fabulous view across a part of Dorset and Somerset known as the Blackmoor Vale, this is 159013 approaching the tunnel with 1L44, the 11.25 Exeter St Davids to London Waterloo service. From this point, the line is on a falling gradient from the tunnel until Templecombe is reached, about five or six miles in the distance. 13 December 2018.

The milepost states 172 miles from London Waterloo and, approaching the current limit of SWR and Class 159 operations is 159002 *City of Salisbury*, arriving at its destination with 1L17, the 08.20 London Waterloo to Exeter St Davids. The rising 1 in 37 gradient between here and Exeter Central is quite evident in this shot. 8 March 2013.

Although the station at Exeter St Davids has remained the same for many years now, the platform numbering and configuration was changed during remodelling in the mid-1980s. 159012 is seen after arriving late from London Waterloo in what was the original departure platform for Southern Railway trains heading for Exeter Central and London Waterloo. After a quick turnaround, it is now about to depart with a late 1L44, the 11.25 Exeter St Davids to London Waterloo. The platform in the foreground on which I was standing was once the main departure platform for Western Region trains heading west, but is now the usual departure platform for Exeter Central and London Waterloo. 17 December 2020.

Passing through the pleasant countryside on the Dorset/Somerset border, this is 159018 + 159103 near Milborne Port, heading west with 1L25, the 10.20 London Waterloo to Exeter St Davids. Out of sight to the right of shot used to be the small station of Milborne Port, which was closed back in the late 1960s but is now a very nice private residence. 8 March 2020.

Very near to the location in the previous picture but heading in the opposite direction, 159020 is leading 1L40, the 10.25 Exeter St Davids to London Waterloo. From the angle of this shot, it looks like the train is on a single line, but it is in fact on a double-track here. 27 August 2009.

Almost-new 159006 is arriving at Sherborne with an unidentified service just four days after the units started working passenger trains to Exeter. Full introduction of Class 159s was not completed until mid-July 1993. It is believed that this unit was the first one to work a passenger service. 10 April 1993.

159022 has just passed Wilton Junction, west of Salisbury leading 1L25, the 10.20 London Waterloo to Exeter St Davids. The lines to the left of shot head off through the Wylye Valley to Warminster and Westbury.
3 April 2015.

Looking west from the bridge from which the previous picture was taken, we see 159013 leading 1L36, the 09.25 Exeter St Davids to London Waterloo service. Just out of sight to the rear of the train is the former Wilton South station, which is now used as private offices.
3 April 2015.

Not long before arriving at Yeovil Junction, this is 159001 *City of Exeter* on the rear of 1L40, the 10.25 Exeter St Davids to London Waterloo. 5 June 2010.

This is the condition all line sides should be in! Massive scrub clearance had just taken place at Pendomer, between Crewkerne and Yeovil Junction, as we see 159010 leading 1L48, the 12.25 Exeter St Davids to London Waterloo.
18 February 2019.

Looking in the other direction from the same bridge as in the last shot, we see 159009 passing through a light shower with a late-running 1L29, the 11.20 London Waterloo to Exeter St Davids.
18 February 2019.

159015 is seen arriving at the 'new' Axminster station at the main down platform with 1L44, the 11.25 Exeter St Davids to London Waterloo train. From the late 1960s to 2009, the station here was reduced to just one platform and a single line. However, after much work to reinstate three miles of track (a so-called 'dynamic loop'), a new footbridge and the reconstruction of the long-closed up platform, it was reopened as a bi-directional station in December 2009. This did create a bit of confusion for passengers, though, as up and down trains could often turn up randomly at either platform! Although the station is still bi-directionally signalled, these days most trains use the appropriate platforms. 21 January 2010.

Back in the days of steam, the area around Honiton Tunnel was a magnet for photographers, due to the gruelling climb for steam locomotives, which in places was as steep as 1 in 80 from the eastern direction. As usual, most of the area is now hopelessly overgrown and decent shots are just about impossible. This is 159020, approaching a bridge about a quarter of a mile from the tunnel with an unidentified westbound service. 19 April 2007.

The bridge from which the last shot was taken can be seen in the background as 159002 *City of Salisbury* leads 1L17, the 08.20 London Waterloo to Exeter St Davids, up the cleared cutting towards Honiton Tunnel. 19 April 2007.

Turning the camera in the other direction, we see 159022 exiting the tunnel at the head of an Exeter St Davids to London Waterloo service. Both this and the previous image were taken with permission as there is no public access to this location. Just recently, this has been the site of landslips, sometimes blocking the line. 19 April 2007.

This is 159004 *Basingstoke & Deane* leading 1L36, the 09.25 Exeter St Davids to London, away from the stop at Honiton. This unit was the first to reach Exeter, way back in early 1993 on a test run. 30 June 2016.

Once again, the inevitable rampant undergrowth has completely transformed this location. 159002 *City of Salisbury* is approaching Feniton with 1L17, the 08.20 London Waterloo to Exeter St Davids train. Many years ago, this once double-tracked main line was bordered by a goods yard and a branch line to Sidmouth on the right, whilst somewhere on the left of the picture was a signal box controlling the area. Latterly known as Sidmouth Junction, the station itself was closed from 1967 until it was reopened in 1971 as Feniton, a name it had carried for a short while after its original opening in 1860. Note the HST stop notices on the left that related to diverted GWR HSTs and now Intercity Express Trains (IETs) which occasionally use the line at times of engineering works. 23 January 2014.

Above: 159005 *West of England Line* is coming over the level crossing at Feniton with 1L44, the 11.25 Exeter St Davids to London Waterloo. With the platform being so close to this crossing, London-bound trains consisting of more than one unit unavoidably foul it when calling. 23 January 2014.

Left: Looking west, we see 159017+159020 approaching Pinhoe on the outskirts of Exeter with 1L36, the 09.25 Exeter St Davids to London Waterloo train. 23 January 2014.

Pinhoe is another station on the line that closed in the late 1960s, only to reopen again in the early 1980s after a public campaign. Viewed from the same bridge as the last shot, 159020 is on the left, departing on the rear of 1L36, the 09.25 Exeter St Davids to London Waterloo seen in the previous shot. Just arrived to the right is 159013 with 1L09, the 07.38 Salisbury to Exeter St Davids. With a long single-line section to Honiton commencing just east of here, this is often a location where London-bound trains from Exeter can be held, waiting for the down service to arrive. 23 January 2014.

Class 159s have not really operated too far from their intended areas, but a few do stray occasionally. To conclude this first chapter, we have a short series of shots of such wanderings. During the SWT era, there were occasional shortages of units, so if a unit was on maintenance, perhaps for work on just the centre coach, it could be removed altogether to make the unit a two-coach set. This was by no means a common occurrence, so I was pleased to see 159001 *City of Exeter*, minus its centre coach, working local circular service 2S19, the 09.07 Romsey to Salisbury (via Eastleigh and Southampton) calling at Millbrook (Hants). 16 January 2004.

Right: Looking west at Millbrook (Hants), we see 159010 approaching with 5Y15, the 13.51 Bournemouth TRSMD to Salisbury TRSMD. This is a semi-regular run that is a returning unit off maintenance at Bournemouth TRSMD. 31 July 2014.

Below: Another unusual location where units are sometimes seen is Winchester, but they are not usually on passenger service. 159002 *City of Salisbury* approaches the station with 5Y21, the 12.20 Basingstoke Barton Mill Carriage Sidings to Salisbury TRSMD, which doubled up as a route-learning trip to keep drivers refreshed on this route for any future diversions from the normal Salisbury to Basingstoke (via Andover) line. I am not sure it still runs nowadays. 17 May 2007.

I have no idea of the reasons behind this working. 159010 is seen taking the Portsmouth line at St Denys. Presumably the unit was heading to Fratton Depot from Salisbury. 26 September 2013.

A driver/route learning run that does operate fairly regularly at the present time is 5Y20, the 10.43 Salisbury Reception Line to Basingstoke Barton Mill Carriage Sidings. It is seen here approaching Shawford, just north of Eastleigh, with 159003 (formerly *Templecombe*) doing the honours. 17 February 2022.

A month earlier, 5Y20 is seen approaching Eastleigh, this time with an immaculate 159001 (formerly *City of Exeter*). Opinions have been divided about the SWR livery, but when it is clean, as it is here, I think it looks rather pleasant. 28 January 2022.

The driver has changed ends and 159008 is just about to depart from Branksome for the last half a mile or so of its journey with 5Y14, the 11.41 Salisbury TRSMD to Bournemouth TRSMD. 15 January 2007.

It is very rare to see a unit on the Great Western Main Line, but this is 159022, the final 159/0 to undergo the latest refurbishment and repainting, heading away from the camera as it passes through Cholsey station on its run from Salisbury TRSMD to Loughborough. It was being driven by a Rail Operations Group (ROG) driver. 18 November 2019.

We have seen a truncated two-car 159 but, for many reasons, it would be highly unlikely to see a one-car unit on the main line! However, an observer stood on Salisbury station platform may occasionally see a sight such as this. Driving coach 57882 of unit 159010 is seen being shunted around in the environs of Salisbury TRSMD under its own power. 8 April 2017.

Finally, our last image in this section is a complete mystery. The initial order of Class 159/0s were numbered from 159001 to 159022 but, try as I might, I can find no reason as to why 159022 is clearly numbered 159023 on the front, despite showing '9022 57894' on the coach side to signify its true identity. Anyhow, what is properly 159022 is entering the depot complex at Bournemouth TRSMD with an open day shuttle service from Bournemouth Central. 17 May 1998.

Chapter 2
Class 159/1

During the mid- to late 2000s, many Class 158 units across the UK became surplus to requirements after being replaced by various types of new units. SWT decided to take on eight of these from Trans Pennine Express, all of which were three-car sets. Refurbished and given SWT livery, they were put back into service during 2007. They were classed as 159/1, as they still had quite a few detail differences from the original 159/0s, not least the slight reduction in engine power.

This is 159101 (formerly 158800) passing Worting Junction with 1L35, the 12.50 London Waterloo to Salisbury service. To date none of the 159/1s has ever carried names or been given SWR livery. 4 December 2012.

Viewed from the opposite direction from the bridge in the previous shot, 159102 (formerly 158803) is approaching with 1L34, the 10.47 Salisbury to London Waterloo. This unit was unfortunately involved in the serious crash at Salisbury Tunnel on 31 October 2021 and was severely damaged, probably never to work again. 13 September 2012.

With the end of SWT workings beyond Exeter St Davids in late 2009, the 159/1s were only seen further west than this for a couple of years. This is 159103 (formerly 158804), soon after departing from Teignmouth with an unidentified service for London Waterloo. 30 August 2008.

159101 waits to depart Newton Abbot with 1L52, the 12.35 Paignton to Waterloo service. This was another station that was a hive of activity many years ago. The area to the right of the picture was once the location of a large steam depot and, later, a diesel depot and associated sidings. 20 September 2008.

A well known vantage point now lost forever is this one at Aller Junction, just west of Newton Abbot. 159108 (formerly 158801) is approaching with an evening Plymouth to London Waterloo service. The former bridge that spanned the lines here, and from which this shot was taken, was demolished to make way for a new road scheme during the mid-2010s. 30 August 2008.

The ill-fated 159102 is seen again, this time approaching Grateley, west of Andover, with 1L29, the 11.20 London Waterloo to Exeter St Davids.
12 December 2013.

Also at Grateley, this is 159105 (formerly 158807) calling with 1L19, the 08.50 London Waterloo to Salisbury service. Back in the mists of time, there was a branch line from here that followed the West of England line for around two and a half miles west until veering off towards Amesbury and Bulford Camp military base. At the time, Amesbury was the closest station for Stonehenge. Unfortunately, this branch was closed to passengers way back in 1952.
1 November 2017.

Gillingham (Dorset) is the location now for 159103, which is arriving with the empty coaching stock (ECS) for 1L30, the 09.18 Gillingham (Dorset) to Basingstoke. The unit had earlier arrived on a terminating service from Basingstoke.
3 September 2015.

The once-busy station at Exeter Central is now very much quieter than in its 1950s and 1960s heyday. Signs of these days gone by are evident in this shot, with the wide distance between the platforms bearing witness to two centre tracks long removed. 159104 (formerly 158805) is seen nearing the end of its journey, calling with 1L17, the 08.20 London Waterloo to Exeter St Davids. 11 September 2017.

On the same day, a sudden shower greets the arrival of 159104 at Exeter Central on its return with 1L48, the 12.25 Exeter St Davids to London Waterloo. The severity of the 1 in 37 gradient can just about be made out by looking back along the train as it curves downwards towards the rear. Surprisingly still standing, the former signal box to the right has been closed since 1970. 11 September 2017.

The end of the up platform at Exeter Central can be seen through the bridge as 159106 (formerly 158809) departs with 1L40, the 10.25 Exeter St Davids to London Waterloo. Again, the view is vastly different from here than it was around sixty years ago, not least because there was a large signal box in the area behind the unit. Out of shot to the left, there also used to be a large carriage shed. 24 March 2011.

Dominating the background on the right in this view is Exeter Prison as 159108 departs with 1L40, the 10.25 Exeter St Davids to London Waterloo. The newer apartment blocks to the left are built on what used to be the quite extensive goods yard. 29 June 2017.

We are now at the other end of the West of England line at Whitchurch (Hants) as 159107 (formerly 158811) arrives, leading an unidentified service heading for Salisbury. This station used to be known as Whitchurch North, to differentiate it from the nearby Whitchurch Town, which was on the Didcot, Newbury and Southampton Line that passed beneath the western end of this station but closed in the early 1960s. 25 January 2015.

Heading south through one of the series of chalk cuttings mentioned in the first chapter, 159102 is leading 1L25, the 10.20 London Waterloo to Exeter St Davids, just west of Whitchurch (Hants). In the background is one of the overbridges that was rebuilt in the early 2010s to accommodate larger boxes on Freightliner Intermodal trains. 21 February 2013.

This location is Ford, on the outskirts of Salisbury, where we see 159105 passing with 1V23, the 09.50 London Waterloo to Yeovil Junction service. The old concrete permanent-way huts are now a rare sight on the modern railway. 23 July 2008.

A couple of wintry shots now. Another of those concrete permanent-way huts features as we see 159103 a mile or so west of Yeovil Junction with 1L29, the 11.20 London Waterloo to Exeter St Davids service. 6 January 2010.

A few years later with more snow in the west country. Here is 159103 again, this time heading south at Motcombe, near Gillingham (Dorset) with a slightly late-running 1L25, the 10.20 London Waterloo to Exeter St Davids. Note in both of these shots the covering over of the coupling, which helps to prevent it from freezing and causing connection problems between units. 18 January 2013.

The first shot of a few workings on former BR Western Region lines now. This image shows 159106 pulling away from Oldfield Park, near Bath, with 1O48, the 12.51 Bristol Temple Meads to Salisbury, which would connect at Salisbury to 1L48, the 12.25 Exeter St Davids to London Waterloo service, for the continuation of its journey. 3 October 2016.

159106 again, this time having just departed Bradford on Avon and approaching the second of two foot-crossings with 1V21, the 10.57 Salisbury to Bristol Temple Meads. This had detached at Salisbury from the rear of 1L21, the 09.20 London Waterloo to Exeter St Davids. 19 February 2010.

159106 is seen yet again some years later, a little further back along the same line as in the previous shot, and with the same service. It is approaching Bradford Junction, from where the single line to Chippenham and Swindon (via Melksham) branches off. 29 September 2016.

A bright autumn afternoon sees 159108 approaching the stop at Westbury with 1O48, the 12.51 Bristol Temple Meads to Salisbury/London Waterloo service. The tracks to the right of picture lead to Heywood Road Junction and the Berks and Hants line to Reading and London Paddington. 21 November 2015.

Now at Westbury station, we see 159103 waiting to depart with 1V33, the 12.20 Waterloo (13.52 Salisbury) to Bristol Temple Meads service. 27 March 2017.

The same service as in the previous image is seen at Westbury again, this time arriving into Platform 1 with 159106 catching a fine glint from the low winter sunshine. 30 December 2014.

Just west of Westbury is Fairwood Junction, another popular vantage point for photography. 159103 is taking the station line with 1O50, the 13.17 Yeovil Junction to London Waterloo. 3 September 2021.

With Bruton station in the distance, 159104 has just departed with 1V35, the 13.50 Waterloo to Yeovil Pen Mill. This service has since stopped running. 9 April 2021.

About a mile south of the previous shot, 159103 is leading a diverted London Waterloo to Exeter St Davids service at Cole. This photograph was taken from a section of embankment that once formed part of the Somerset and Dorset Railway, which passed over the Western Region line at this point until its closure in 1966. 20 September 2015.

Above: Viewed from the same location as the last shot but from the other direction, 159103 is seen again thanks to a 'window' in the vegetation providing a good frame for the unit which is approaching with a Yeovil Junction to London Waterloo service. 14 July 2019.

Left: This is 159108 at Heytesbury, just east of Warminster on the line to Salisbury, with a Bristol Temple Meads to London Waterloo service. 25 September 2012.

On the same line as in the last shot but this time nearer to Salisbury, this is 159105 with an unidentified service heading for Salisbury. It is passing the site of Wilton North station, closed as long ago as 1955 but, almost 70 years on, still showing evidence of a platform in the undergrowth just beyond the bridge in the distance. There have even been rumblings over the years about the reopening of a new station near to here, but they have come to nothing so far. 3 April 2015.

We are now back on the unit's normal operating route for the last series of shots and the conclusion of this book. 159102 is around five minutes or so into its journey as it passes Vauxhall with the 11.50 London Waterloo to Salisbury service. Note that a few of the 159/1s retained the small snowplough attachment on the front skirting from their days as Class 158s.
17 October 2012.

159103 is heading west through the busy section of line at Wimbledon West Junction with the 09.50 London Waterloo to Salisbury train. Many of these trains to/from London that terminate at Salisbury are, at the present time (2023), cut back to start or terminate at Basingstoke.
17 October 2012.

On a miserable, drizzly day, this is 159104 leading 1L25, the 10.20 London Waterloo to Exeter St Davids, through Brookwood.
1 March 2022.

159101 is travelling east through Fleet at its maximum top speed of 90mph, with 1L34, the 10.47 Salisbury to London Waterloo service. The construction of a large multistorey car park here a few years ago has made this viewpoint possible. 11 November 2016.

Not far from the location in the previous shot, 159107 leads 1L26, the 06.40 Exeter St Davids to London Waterloo service, through Winchfield. In recent times, the wide space between the tracks at this location has become a mini forest! 23 September 2016.

Just east of Farnborough (Main), a very convenient footbridge crosses the line, providing good views in each direction. This is 159103, leading another 159 and a 158 as 1L21, the 09.20 London Waterloo to Exeter St Davids. The Class 158 would have come off the rear at Salisbury to form a service to Bristol Temple Meads. 6 June 2016.

Looking in the opposite direction towards Farnborough (Main) station, we see a very clean 159104, again running at its maximum permitted speed of 90mph, passing with 1L30, the 09.18 Gillingham (Dorset) to London Waterloo service. This is another one of the services that has since been cut back to terminate at Basingstoke. 6 June 2016.

Our last view from this footbridge sees a telephoto shot that emphasises the reverse curves here. Farnborough (Main) station can be seen through the bridge as 159105 leads a Class 158 with 1L24, the 07.11 Yeovil Pen Mill to London Waterloo (via Sherborne) service. 12 September 2019.

Basingstoke is a good location to observe the 159s. If memory serves me correctly, this is the first working of a newly converted 159/1, with 159102 on the rear of 1L29. This is the 11.20 London Waterloo to Exeter St Davids, despite the info screen above the cab window stating Yeovil Junction. The unit was detached at Salisbury, I believe, with the leading unit continuing to Exeter St Davids. 5 December 2006.

For some years now, the main departure platform at Salisbury for West of England line trains has been number 3, but this one was originally Platform 4. Platform 3 served cross-country services from Portsmouth to Bristol and Cardiff, but both of these are now interchangeable (and bi-directional). This is 159108 waiting to depart with 1L21, the 09.20 London Waterloo to Exeter St Davids. Upon departure of this train, the rear unit would then leave for Bristol Temple Meads, forming a working that has now finished. 23 September 2019.

This time we are at Farnborough (Main) station to see 159108 passing through with 1L30, the 09.18 Gillingham (Dorset) to London Waterloo service. 9 December 2015.

Above: Immaculate 159104 is seen making its debut after conversion from 158805 at Salisbury as it heads on to the depot along with a Class 158 during a shunt move. 7 February 2007.

Right: The old freight/parcels dock at Basingstoke is now a car park and makes a fine viewpoint for trains approaching from the London direction. This is 159104, leading 1L37, the 13.20 London Waterloo to Exeter St Davids service past 159007 stabled in the siding to the right. 16 December 2011.

159107 approaches Platform 2 with 1L35, the 12.50 London Waterloo to Salisbury. At the time of writing, this train now starts from here rather than Waterloo. 8 January 2016.

159101 is departing Platform 2 at Basingstoke with the same train as in the previous shot. 6 August 2015.

Led by 159104, this nine-car formation departs east from Basingstoke with 1L24, the 07.11 Yeovil Pen Mill to London Waterloo service. This is another example that has the mini snowplough on the front skirting from its days as a Class 158. 20 July 2020.

Although it is early December, this is a very autumnal scene at Andover. 159106 leads a Class 158 arriving with 1L29, the 11.20 London Waterloo to Exeter St Davids. The overgrown area between the tracks was once the site of two through lines, long since removed. 4 December 2013.

This is the view from the road bridge seen in the distance of the previous shot. 159104 leads 1L35, the 12.50 London Waterloo to Salisbury, away from Andover. Network Rail's use of the hideously ugly palisade fencing is all too obvious here. It wouldn't be so bad if it were at least a darker colour! In the last few years, a huge multistorey car park has been erected to the right of the picture. 15 March 2014.

The wide space between the tracks at Andover is seen again, looking somewhat less overgrown this time! 159106 is departing with 1L44, the 11.25 Exeter St Davids to London Waterloo. 1 December 2011.

We now head west again to see 159108 approaching Tisbury with a Yeovil Junction to London Waterloo service. This was a tricky bridge to get to; I had to cross a small stream and a very muddy field! 9 July 2012.

Just west beyond Tisbury is the small hamlet of West Hatch, where we see 159102 leading 1L25, the 10.20 London Waterloo to Exeter St Davids. When it was refurbished by SWT (just prior to the SWR takeover), this was one of just a couple of examples of 159/1s to have the colour from the cab area finished in a series of points rather than being plain. 8 July 2017.

Taken from the same bridge at West Hatch, we see 159107 approaching from the opposite direction, leading 1L40, the 10.25 Exeter St Davids to London Waterloo. 8 July 2017.

159105 is seen at Tisbury, departing on the rear of 1L17, the 08.20 London Waterloo to Exeter St Davids. As with many locations on the West of England line, rumours have been going around for many years about the reinstatement of double track and the former down platform (from which I took this shot) but again, nothing has ever come of it.
23 September 2017.

Approaching a foot crossing near Semley, 159101 makes an imposing view as it negotiates the reverse curves. It is leading a late-running 1L29, the 11.20 London Waterloo to Exeter St Davids service.
9 July 2017.

A shot taken at the same spot but later in the afternoon on a different day, this is 159105 leading 1L45, the 15.20 London Waterloo to Exeter St Davids. At this point, the train is on a rising gradient, which was always quite a challenge for steam crews in days gone by.
8 September 2014.

A dull December day sees newly converted 159102 leading 1L52, the 13.25 Exeter St Davids to London Waterloo, away from Yeovil Junction. The train is passing over the Yeovil Pen Mill to Weymouth line, whilst just visible above it is the line that leads from Yeovil Junction to Yeovil Pen Mill. The semaphore signals just discernible were replaced by colour lights some years ago. 14 December 2006.

Arriving at what is now the main up platform, this is 159107 with 1L58, the 15.44 Yeovil Pen Mill to London Waterloo, which had arrived at Yeovil Pen Mill as 1V35, the 13.50 London Waterloo to Yeovil Pen Mill. Neither of these trains runs any longer, unfortunately. 13 April 2018.

This is 159103 at Yeovil Junction with 1L25, the 10.20 London Waterloo to Exeter St Davids. The former down platform on which I was standing is now used by the Yeovil Railway Centre and occasionally hosts charter trains and sometimes engineers' trains. The former down fast line has been retained to facilitate locomotive run-rounds. The truncated footbridge in the left of the background originally spanned all lines to serve the down platform. 27 February 2019.

The rather impressive-looking station clock at Yeovil Junction is showing that 159104, with the 1O56 14.51 Yeovil Junction to London Waterloo, is slightly overdue. This is currently one of a couple of trains throughout the day that travel via Westbury to Salisbury, and then on to London Waterloo. 9 July 2019.

On a day of sunshine and (mostly!) showers, we see 159105 leading 1L40, the 10.25 Exeter St Davids to London Waterloo service, at Pendomer, around five miles or so west of Yeovil Junction. This shot would have been impossible in the many years prior to this date, as the cutting sides were covered with trees to the size of rainforest proportions. 18 February 2019.

To bring this book to a close, we bear witness to the closure of Gillingham (Dorset) signal box, with the legend in the window saying it all. Just two days after this image was taken, the box was closed and all control of the area passed to Basingstoke. However, it has been retained as a ground frame for the permanent-way department to occasionally operate the siding points seen in the foreground of this shot. 159104 is seen pulling away with 1L41, the 14.20 London Waterloo to Exeter St Davids, whilst in the up platform is 159021 with 1L58, the 16.18 Gillingham (Dorset) to Basingstoke service. 24 February 2012.

Other books you might like:

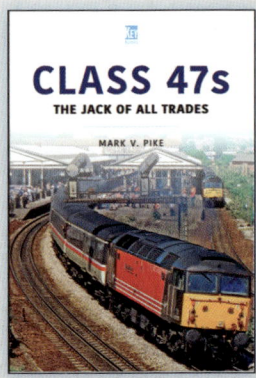

Britain's Railways Series, Vol. 45

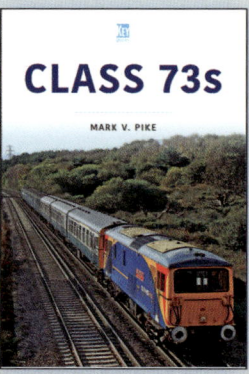

Britain's Railways Series, Vol. 41

Britain's Railways Series, Vol. 39

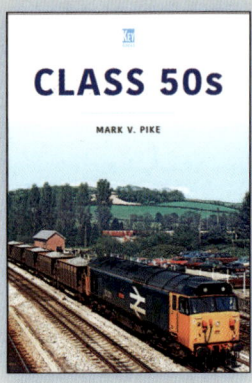

Britain's Railways Series, Vol. 36

Britain's Railways Series, Vol. 35

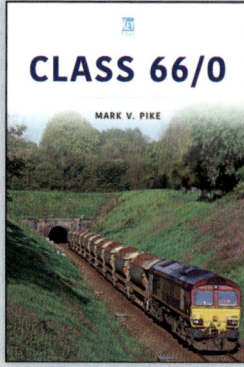

Britain's Railways Series, Vol. 32

For our full range of titles please visit:
shop.keypublishing.com/books

VIP Book Club

Sign up today and receive
TWO FREE E-BOOKS

Be the first to find out about our forthcoming book releases and receive exclusive offers.

Register now at **keypublishing.com/vip-book-club**

Our VIP Book Club is a 100% spam-free zone, and we will never share your email with anyone else.
You can read our full privacy policy at: privacy.keypublishing.com